Baba D

The Great Hug Me Too

ISBN: 978-0-9952444-0-5

Copyright Donna Pidlubny 2016
Published by Home Free
Toronto, Ontario, Canada

This is a Poogaloo
Muppy-gum-shoe
Who lives in the land
Of the Hullaballoo

This is a Poogaloo

Muppy-gum-shoe

Who lives in the land

Of the HullAballoo

This is the mighty
Oo-too-boom-bay
Who lives uptown
Where the Hugalumps play

This

is

the

MIGHTY

Oo-
too-
BOOM-
bay

Who lives uptown

Where the Hugalumps play

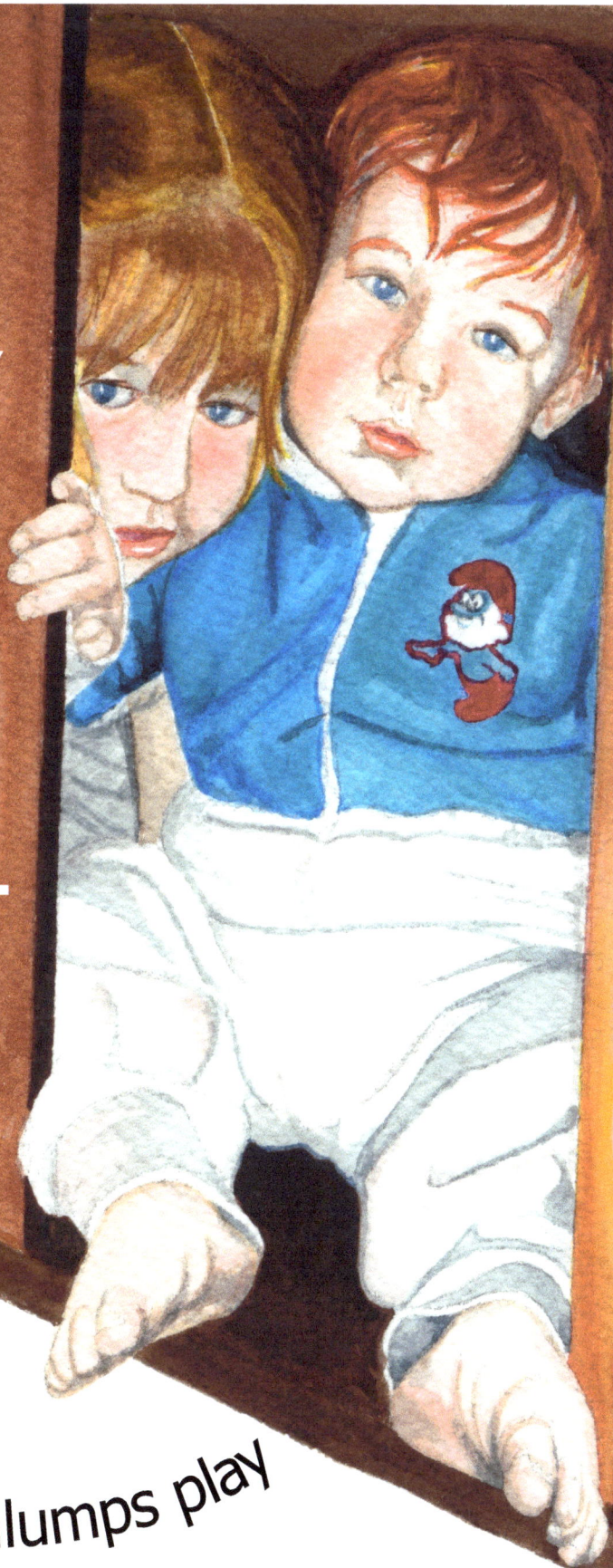

These are the teensie
Ricki-tin-tee
Who chase the rivers
of Razzamaree

These are the teensie Ricki-tin-tee

Who chase the rivers of RazzAmaree

This is the awesome
Pa-na-man-droo
Who stalks the mountains
Of Moo-moo-man-doo

This is the awesome

Pa-na-man-droo

Who stalks the mountains

Of Moo-moo-man-doo

This is the smiley
Giggle-a-way
Who sniggles the sun
With a hooperumhay

This is the smiley

Giggle-a-way

Who sniggles the sun

with a hooperumhay

This is the noisy
Boogle-ba-ram
Who lives on a railroad
In Marakazam

This is the noisY

Boogle-ba-ram

In Marakazam

Who lives on a railroad

This is the Strawnary
Ninji-ka-room
Who makes her bed
On the closet broom

This is the Strawnary

Ninji-ka-room

Who makes her bed On the closet broom

This is the terrible
Koo-koo-kon-shoo
Who falls on her face
When you say a-choo

This is the terrible Koo-koo-kon-shoo

Who falls on her face

When you say

a-choo

This is the beautiful
Oola-fan-chay
Who floats on a fringle
In Salacambay

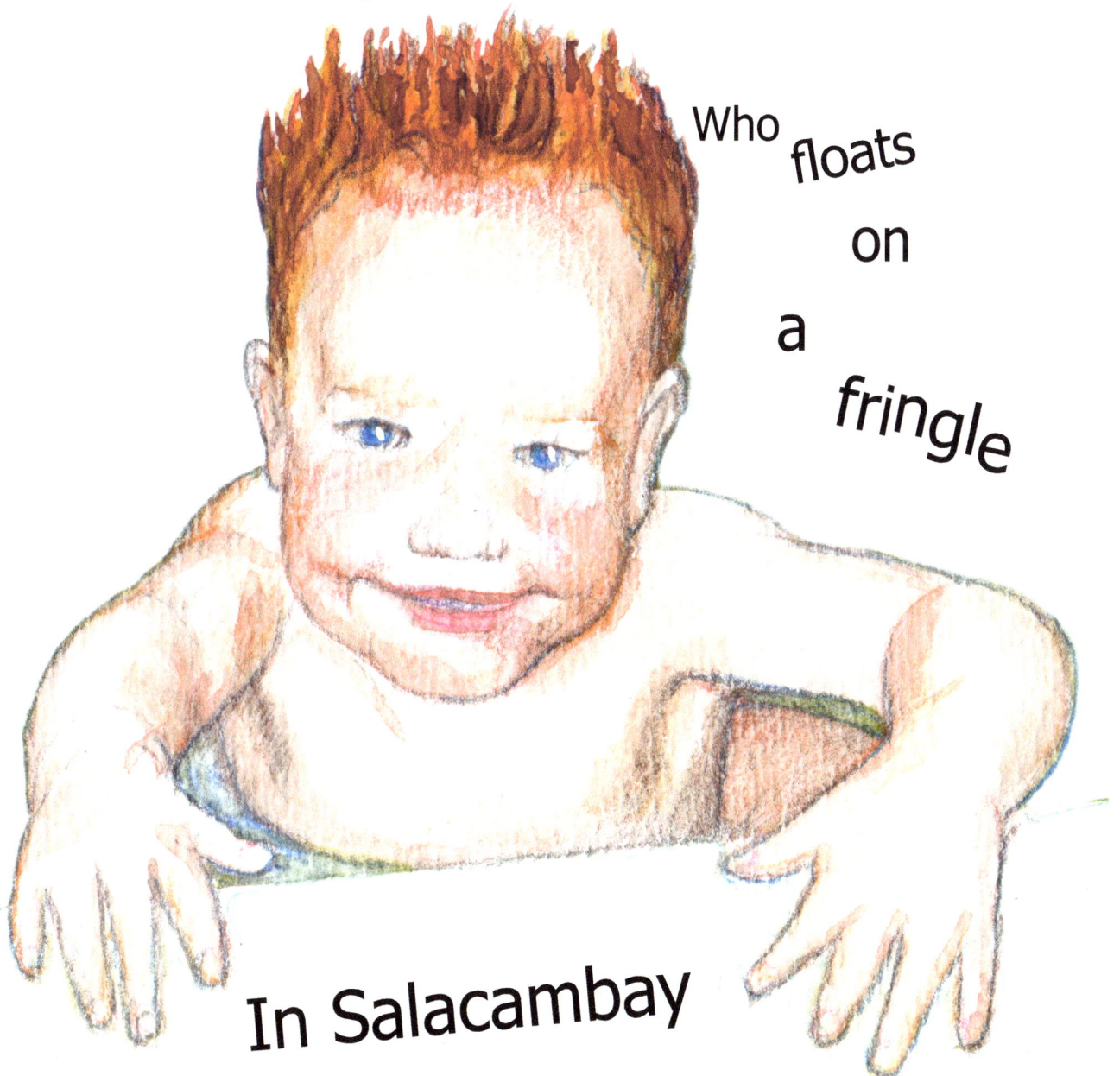

This
is
*the*beautiful

Oola-fan-chay

Who floats

on

a

fringle

In Salacambay

These are the Flibbers
Who sing with their toes
And live in a land
Where the willigrass grows

These are the Flibbers   Who sing with their toes

And live in a land

Where the willigrass grows

This is the Fliberty
Peri-gan-oon
Who swings on the chin
Of the Man-in-the-Moon

This is the Fliberty
Peri-gan-oon
Who swings on the chin
Of the Man-in-the-Moon

This is the squeaky
Mimi-van-blick
Who squeadles her beadles
And lives on a stick

This is the squeaky Mimi-van-blick

Who squeadles her beadles

And lives on a stick

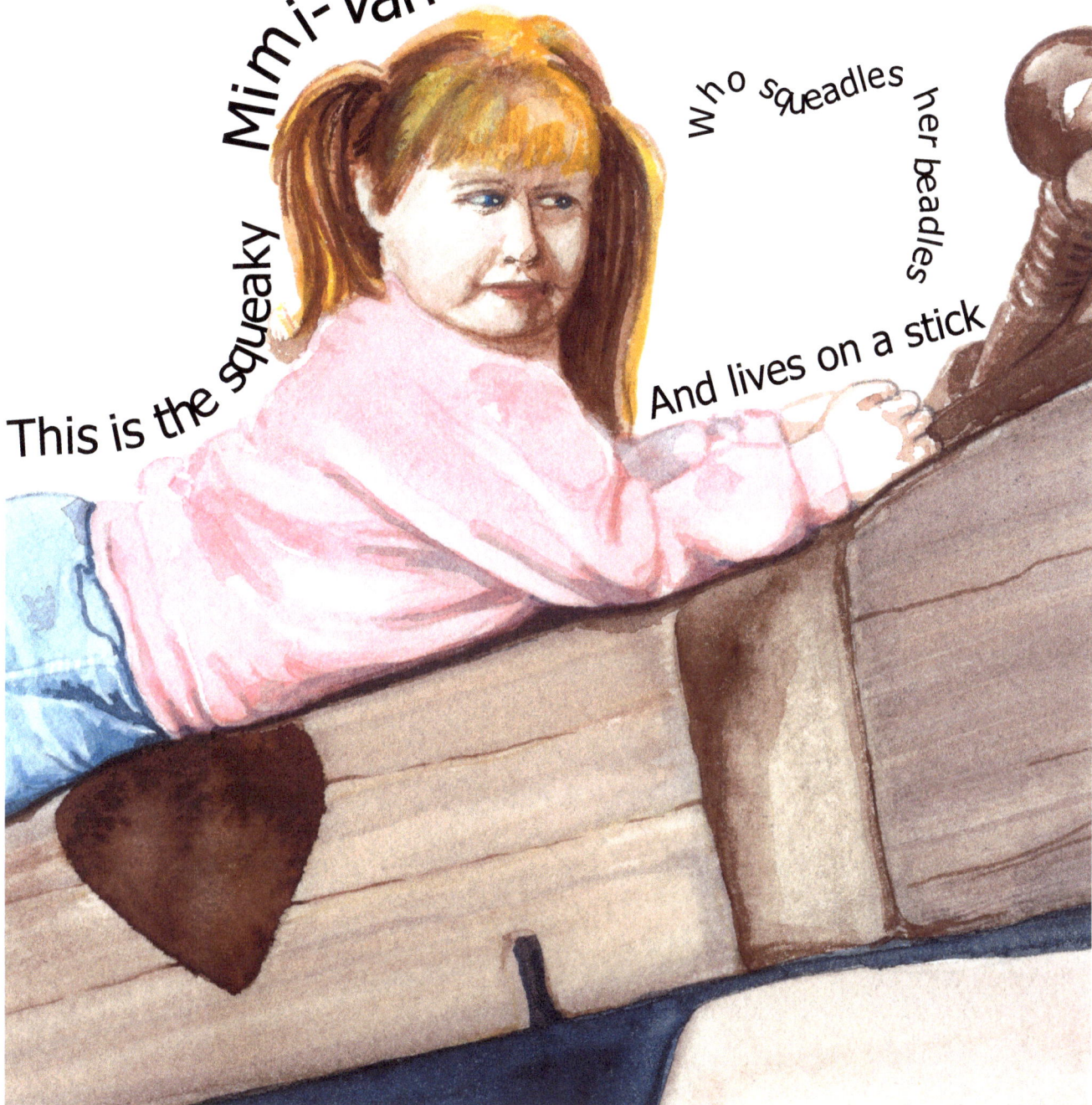

This is the uggerly
Figger-um-dode
Who lives with the looloos
Just down the road

This is the uggerly

Figger-um-dode

Who
lives
with
the
looloos

Just down the road

This is a Priggle
All meemsie and wan
Who frets and foroomigates
All the day long

This is a Priggle

All meemsie and wan

Who frets and foroomigates

All the day long

This is the warlike
Ringa-jin-thing
With great big moustaches
Four eyes and no chin

This is the warlike
Ringa-jin-thing
With great big moustaches
Four eyes and no chin

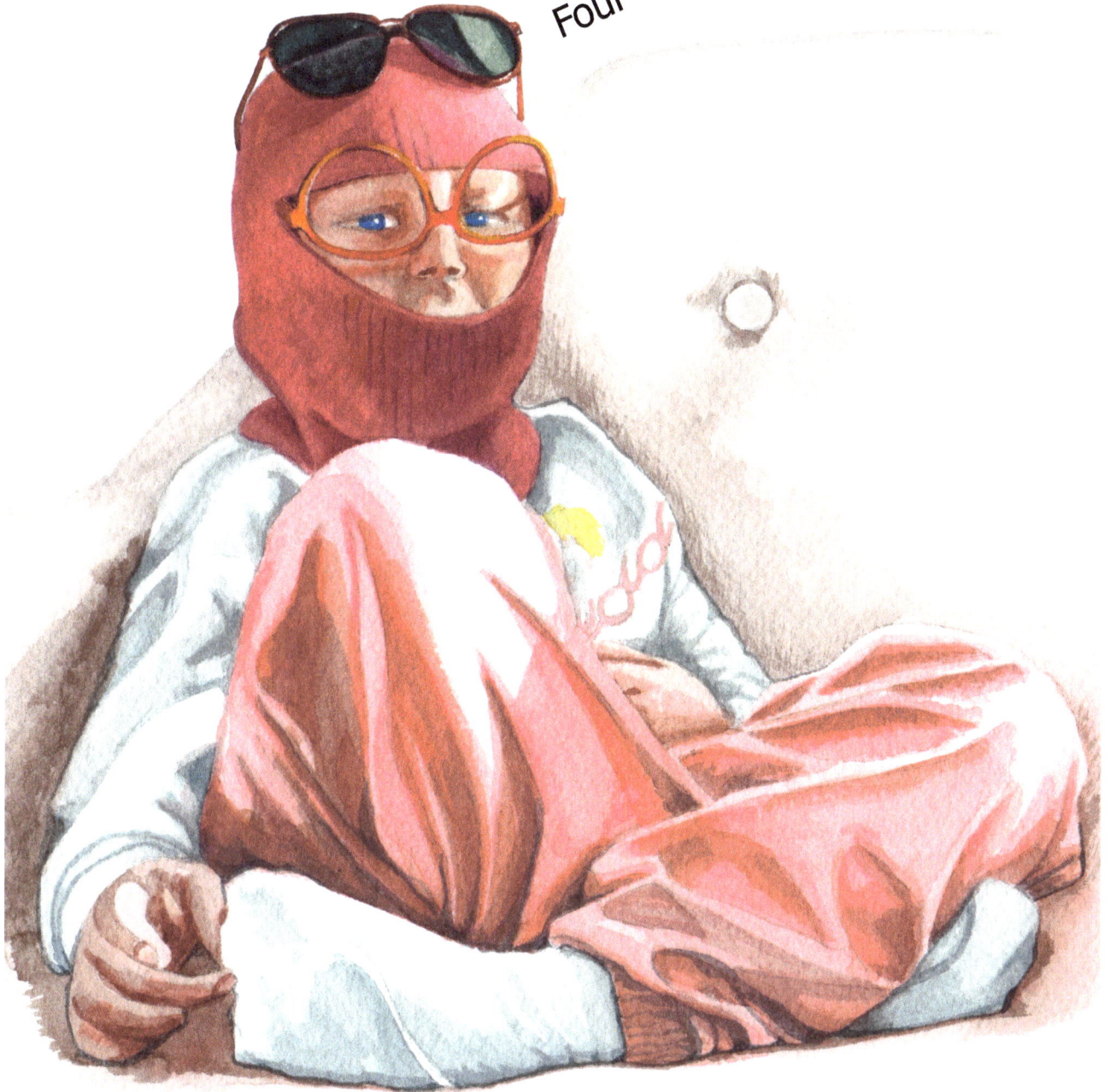

This is the Flooky
Flimmy-ram-sham
Who oogles the redges
In strawberry jam

This is the Fl$_{oo}$ky
Flimmy-RAM-sham

Who OOgles the redges

In strawberry jam

This is a basseous
Shining Garoo
Who dances on top
Of the Toocan balloo

This is a basseous SHINING GAROO who dances on top

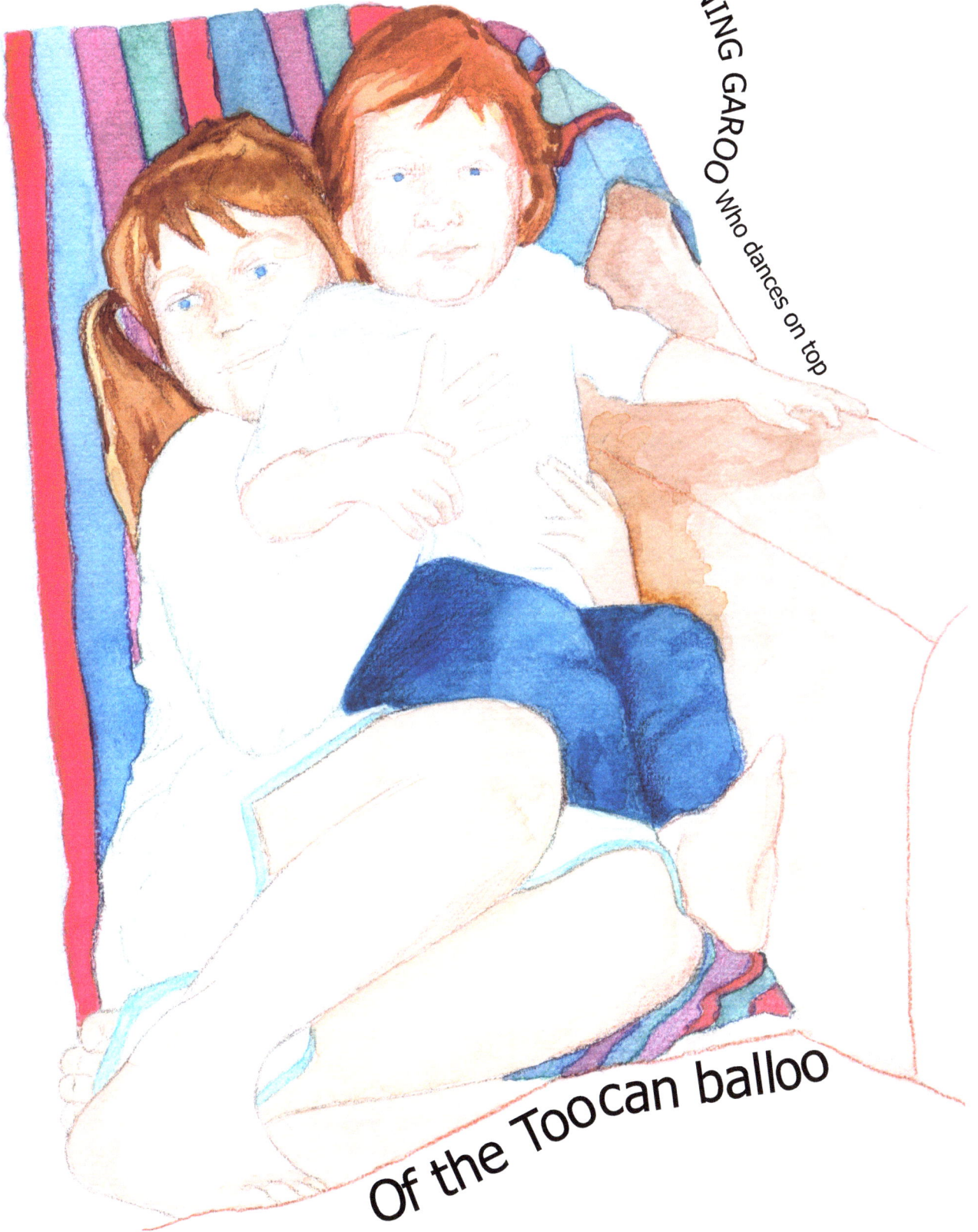

Of the Toocan balloo

This is the squishy
Omar-carrump
Who hides under carpets
And snoodles her trump

This is the squi^{is}h_y
Omar-carrUMP

Who hides under carpets

And snoodles her trump

This is me
I'm a Cherry-chin-choo
With a voice like thunder
When I call you

This is me

I'm a **CHERRY-CHIN-CHOO**

With a voice like **thunder**

When I call you

And this is you
The Great Hug-Me-Too
Who snuggles and snoozes and
smiles and canoozes
And twirles on the tips of the
terripaloozes
And says to the thundering
Cherry-chin-choo
Here I am, Here I am,
HUG-ME-TOO!

And this is you **The Great Hug-Me-Too**

Who snuggles
and snoozes
and smiles
and canoozes

And twirls
on the tips
of the
terripaloozes

And says to the thundering

Cherry-chin-choo

Here I am, Here I am,
HUG-ME-TOO!

Inspiration comes by many paths. Sometimes it's in the words of a friend. Other times it's in a smile from a child at play. Many thanks to my long time friend Dilys Buchan, who offered the words that fueled my imagination. And to my children Adrienne and Samantha, who filled my days with laughter, joy, and endless challenges. But mostly for teaching me how to love unconditionally.

www.ingramcontent.com/pod-product-compliance
Lightning Source LLC
Chambersburg PA
CBHW042101040426
42448CB00002B/89